THAT WAS
UNEXPECTED

KARSTEN COLBERT

Fulton Books, Inc.
Meadville, PA

Published by Fulton Books 2020

ISBN 978-1-64654-273-4 (paperback)
ISBN 978-1-64654-274-1 (digital)

Printed in the United States of America

In My Hour of Need

I am not ashamed to bend the knee
and on bending knee is where I stand my ground
on my knees I pray toward the sun that makes my shadow starts to sway
I'm dancing in the shadows of the dying day where others peer to create and put up brick walls to keep others away
I say with my hands up still dancing alone that I am a bullet
I am a bullet from time to time I stray
I can feel myself when I go weightless
I can feel others pulling and tugging and throwing me with their minds full of negative thoughts in directions that I should not be, but here is where I make my stand on bending knee
I demand that you surrender your selfish needs and allow them to clash with mine so that we can rescue one another in my hour of need

Hold

I want to hold you
I want to slide inside you
I want to hold your face and slowly kiss you
I need to look forward into your eyes to see the real you
I need you and our rhythm to keep moving with the same time
I want you
No,
I need you to feel that I'm free with you
Hold fast
Hold on
I just need to hold to you

Reality

Rain is falling
I'm looking at photographs of you,
Wishing you were here
As you walk in the room, you whispered in my ear that I had
this coming
You take your fingers and slide your nails under the top and
bottom buttons of my shirt
I want to be with you, but not now
My behavior is unacceptable, I do
I don't
What's wrong with me?
It's a miracle that you want to be with me
You become very physical as you push me to the ground
It's clear in my head
That I'm immobilize by the thought of you, paralyze by the
sight of you,
Hypnotize by the words you say
I'm just an innocent, helpless victim
I'm full of regret because I want you so much we begin kissing
We are somewhere beyond happiness and sadness
We're just as far as eternity

It's heaven
Your clinching your pillow in a naked sweat, and I've been the needle and thread
Waving figure eights in circles around your head as I enjoy the taste you leave in my mouth
I see the outline of your shadow pushing forward and arcing back then it ends
We just sit there in each others arms we watch the sunrise
Then it comes to me
It's only a dream
It's not reality

Sidenote

I constantly repeat your name over and over again in the hollow hallways of my brain, so when I think of you, it sounds like echoes, but it never drives me insane.

Thirst

When I first saw you,
It woke me
When I looked in your eyes,
It inspires me
When I smell your sense
It reminds me
That I'm still stuck in the desert at this oasis
When I dream of you,
It scares me
When I think of you,
It overwhelms me
When I'm not around you,
It chokes me
I'm in the middle of this ocean and I can't swim
I saw you
Yeah, I looked
I smelled you
And I was struck by lightning and I couldn't move
I'm thinking about dreaming of you when you're not around
I don't even know you but I want you
I didn't know that you exist
Crazy for this very reason, I'm trying to get close to you
You somehow have become the air that I breathe
You somehow have become life itself
The passion, the hunger, the torture, the love, the hate, the
sanity, the mother, the father, the sun, the moon, the earth
Please come back and breathe life into me

Okay

There are so many things not to say, more things not to say than things to say,
more things that we don't understand than things that we can understand
So we try to dig through with our hands, bleeding, trying to make our way to the truth, but it's so misleading
The number of things that we should care about, we don't care about, but who's to tell us what we should care about?
We find ourselves trying to build ourselves up, so we build our own walls around us, hoping that there is no one that can find the keys to that machine,
praying that no one really sees what we wear on our sleeves
So we call a truce so we can attempt to find the truth from all the lies that we created just so we can get by off our own demons that we've created inside
Maybe I'm rambling on or maybe that's just life because it carries on

Sidenote 4

I've relapsed again
I'm holding my phone,
Staring at pictures of you,
Lost in a daydream,
Dreaming of you and what should've been.

Sin Eater

I speak for the voiceless
I'm here so that she could be here I speak these words
They are more valuable than life itself
I declare my own life in exchange for hers
In exchange for every wrong that she has done
Take all my rights and make her all right
Allow me to eat her sins so that she has no more
I'll carry them on my back in my bag,
In my heart
So that she feels the burden no more
Allow me to take her dagger
Place it down and throw myself upon it
At this moment I am at the wheel of your judgment
Please spin it and allow what I asked to be true
She has no need to know the victory of my lover
For her I'll sit here and allow the sin to devour me
Just so I can set your love free

Sidenote 3

I wish I didn't know where you stand
You're on the beach, looking out to sea
I'm alone on a raft
A drift at sea in front of you but so transparent that you can see

Sidenote 2

Stay strong
for you can do every single thing in your life right
go out of your way
for every person there will always be something to put you down
remember Jesus died helping people

Sideline

Eerie whispers
that scares the hell out of me
are telling me that my last chance has arrived
don't kid yourself, you'll never catch her eye, screaming out that
she's a contradiction
I want to break the spell that she has created
now spread a sense of urgency
I'll declare this an emergency
that without her that would be the death of me
I'll sell her bad memories
and I'll promise to hold her close
'cause I want her like I never wanted anything before I let my
anger rise as he holds her
the same way I want her name
yes, she has a name but I'll never tell
I only dream of my beautiful
I want her to squeeze the life out of me
I always dream of her and she'll never know I want her to suck
the life out of me
now there's nowhere left to hide the truth burns deep inside
and will never die
eerie whispers that scares the hell out of me are telling me that
my last chance has arrived

Read Between the Lines

I have done my research but please, in turn,
Don't ask me for my discovery
Don't ask me why my eyes dissect every picture of you
So my brain can process every inch of you
Because honestly you are the greatest discovery in history
So I escaped in my poems
Because it's my sanctuary from telling the truth, so please don't
ask me if this is about you
Instead read every line of this poem
That I give to you
Like don't ask me if you're beautiful because you're gorgeous
Like don't ask me if you have flaws because you're flawless
Like don't ask me what I'm thinking because I thirst for you
And like a fine wine you are, I want a taste of you
Like I want my fingertips to go on a journey
On your body for a lifetime
Like I want to laugh with you like I want to share with you
Like I want our hearts to play the same rhythm of the same beat
To the same song
And it could if I'm with you
Like I want you to trust me
Turn around trust fall
Do you feel free
To allow me to hold you,
To thrill you?
You, you, you already know
So please don't read between the lines

LOS RECHAZADOS

The Rejects

Silhouettes,
We're only silhouettes of pretty family
Who are you in the silhouette?
The bastard son
Or the one with the suicide ego?
Are you insane,
Alone, sitting in the corner, licking your wounds?
Forgive me, Father,
for my curse of not fitting in of being stupid and fat
for you see I wish that I was gifted, but I'm sick of trying
I'm a stranger in my own family
I feel naked,
like I let you steal my body and soul, like you polish my thoughts
and then my heart explodes
How dare you knock me over and put cement in my veins?
You're just here to watch me burn because you're never satisfied
You're mean, angry, fake, stupid, and cold
But I'm reckless and twisted, sick, and mental
I'm one of the rejects, so here's my time
I'll buy back my soul
With these words you hear, but you will never know

The Nameless

Can you take me as I am cuts on my head,
Cuts on my feet
I can't get you out of my head
You're deep in my skin
You're the splinter in me
You are the ocean and I am a wave
You're in my head tormenting me
Come closer inside
There's something I need you to see
I'll whisper in your ear
Just relax,
You seem rather fragile just like a myth that I have to believe in,
A song that no one sings
You are everything to me
I'll do anything to have you to myself
I've come so you can know me
I'm here to make you proud
In just one night, you will watch as the stars collide as you're lifted from your burdens
Now I just want to trade a question mark in for a maybe because we could be a start that has no end

Sidenote 17

Happiness is just like a thought
It comes and it goes

Harmony

Before you, I saw the world in black and white,
hesitant to understand what was in front of my eyesight instead
of perceiving what was real
my eyes were seeing only the stills of the negatives of the world
After you,
I started to walk into areas of gray now thanks to you
I see the world in blues
The yin and the yang

Sidenote 16

I love you
for all the things
you never discovered about yourself

Phoenix

You are the phoenix
that grew from the broken concrete of the city
out of the flames with the wind blowing over the ashes
You are the phoenix
building your beauty from within
The strength that is in your heart and your soul
The phoenix,
that's what you are, spreading your wings, catching the wind,
and soaring higher then any cloud could ever perceive to want
to be
Your beauty is the key to unlock the door
of the heavenly gates that were created by the creator himself
Phoenix
You are the phoenix

Sidenote 15

We can't do anything because of fear
Fear is our enemy
Once you make fear your ally, your friend,
Then fear no longer has power over you

Flowers on Mother's Day

My grandfather told me that my mother could fly
That on those times, when I barely escaped danger, she swooped
in to rescue me
But why do we gift flowers for Mother's Day?
They die
My grandfather told me that my mother had eyes in the back
of her head
Those days where she can see my actions when washing the
dishes
But why do we gift flowers for Mother's Day?
They die
My grandfather told me that my mother could sense things
There were times that she can sense things and speak to me
without a sound
But why do we gift flowers on Mother's Day?
They die
My grandfather told me that my mother was a world
She was the giver of life, the creator of food, a shoulder to cry
on, a teacher,
A leader,
A gifted healer,
A world building beacon of hope
My grandfather told me that we give our mothers flowers on
Mother's Day to remind us how precious life is while we wait
for their graduation from this life so we can attempt to live up
to their legend

Sidenote 13

I no longer give in to your negativity
Instead I stand on the clouds
Like a giant dancing in my positivity

Can I Tell You Something

Black girl, black girl, your smile is as upside down as a frown
you look as though the world is on your shoulders,
like if you don't find the correct way to walk, your back will bend
and bow from all the stress that has taken
you walk with a purpose like your destination is just around the
corner
you don't turn your head to look to the left because there's danger
you don't turn your head to the right to look because of the
negative
instead you walk with the understanding that every step is on
purpose
your smile reminds me that there is bad in the world
but the look in your eyes tells me that everything will be fine
Okay, you don't need to say the words because they bleed from
you
I smell the truth on you, like it's embedded in your essence but
your smile still seems corrupt
because in your mind, you know there is so much to endure but
never to ignore the ignorance of the world
so when they come back at you, you put your hands up, bobbing
and weaving like a boxer
your gloves are always on for the fight of your life
fingers always in the holster, cocked ready and loaded to go to
tell your truth to throw them off into the world
because the world needs it like
it needs you
black girl, black girl, your smile is as upside down as a frown and
I wish I knew where you find the strength to keep it together

Sidenote 12

Because of our selfish needs and wants, we become and create shitty people

Truth Be Told

God made you to love yourself before me
God made you to understand your worth
God made you with no limits to try to create new outcomes for yourself,
New edges to be molded into better circles to find yourself back to who you are
God made you to love the skin that you're in because if you don't love your own skin, you'll never understand the touch of mine
Truth be told, God made you walk out to the edge that you're afraid of to look out and discover a brand-new you because you cannot love another if you do not love you first

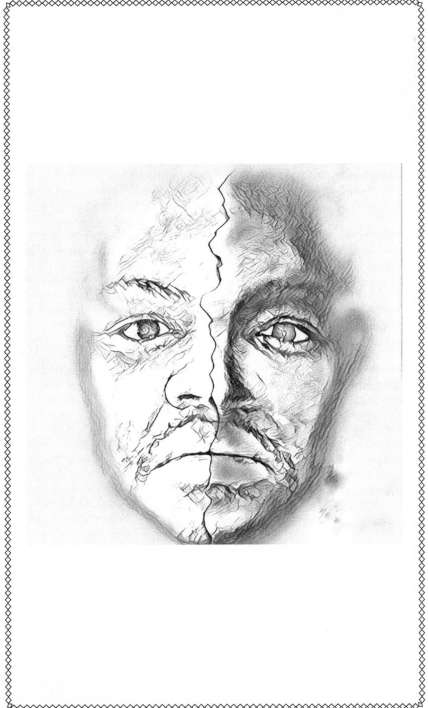

Answer

Answer,
You're determined to find an answer
answer to what
hate, pain,
it's hope,
right, hope is out of season
the pain was too much
it peeled me from the inside, it peeled me from my skin, tear
me from myself,
you're all brainwashed
just give up,
don't be afraid
you're by yourself alone, just lost sight of everything
nothing, you're no one,
just a lost memory rejected from the world,
just a few seconds away from me
I have compromised
I have given in
I still wrestle with my demons but they're winning
I'm here left with a heart exhausted
when they tell me to eat a bullet, I surrender, so can you save
me from myself?

No,
you pull me up just to push me down
What have I done?
the world is killing itself
no hint of life
killing itself, so dark and so cold
killing itself, do you care?
killing itself, nobody cares, so just go
killing itself, let go
killing itself, let go
killing itself, let go
my dreams to wash you all away is upon you
so get busy living or get busy dying

Wish

I wish I could just
I wish I could just be
I wish I could just be with you
I'm saying those words over and over but they're not truth
Truth is, I see you standing, floating on an iceberg
I'm on land and I can't reach you because of her
She's in front of me
A giant wall that I can't break through
I wish, I wish I could just be with you

Facially Challenged

Hello, I am a two. Nice to meet you on the man scale.

1. Ugly
2. Facially challenged
3. Okay
4. Doable
5. OMG

You know, just a two, nothing special, nothing more, nothing less
Just a person that women can talk to sometimes, to be considered a little emotional
You know, it's fine, though
It's okay, I accepted it
Just a buffer for all my other friends
For my friends who are okay and doable, how about the one that is adorable?
The five
The one that women look at him
He's a magnet of their attention
No, I'm not sad
Even though I go home and sit in the shower
And I cry with the water so you don't see the bags under my eyes
Instead I pick up a pad and a pen, and I pour my emotions out on it
So, so sad, so much pain
Just want to be with the girl that you bought three drinks
For then she asked you, "What's your friend's name?"

But bro code allowed you to step aside
It's okay
It's fine
I'm just going to go home
And sit in front of the TV and watch *The Notebook*
I watch *The Lucky One*
Alone
And I'll go to the movies alone
You know, the more I explain, the more it seems crazy,
Depressing
However, it's not
It's just the life of a tow
I'm Mr. Facially Challenged
How about you?

You and I Both

You want to feel something, anything,
Anything more than what you felt with every other person
That you were with before me when you ignored me
I only want to feel you, all over you
Trace the outline of your body, like that's what I need to do with
my tongue
I'm chasing,
Sweat is falling off you
You are finally letting go tonight
You were in a place that you never knew
That you would be before
You're not alone there
I'm beside you
You—no, me,
We both are existing together
Our bodies are sequenced together, moving to a pace
Only you and I know
The feeling that is showing off both of us to a new glow
You bite your lip
And enjoy the movement of passion
That you have never experienced into
Now I keep licking my lips,
Trying to wonder to myself
The taste that you leave in my mouth what it reminds me of
Because you are the single greatest thing that's been on my
tongue

That's when it happens
You are inside of yourself, feeling yourself
You can see the universe
And all the things around it
You can see stars supernova
You just had an outer-body experience and the whole time I'm
thinking to myself, why did we wait so long to see ecstasy?

What Goes Up

When you tell someone you love them, ultimately, you're leaving yourself open for the first punch
You're vulnerable
You're telling them something that you've been holding inside for a long time,
A short time
You're showing them your emotions, letting them in on a secret
That you keep locked tight,
Something that you keep in a lockbox with three guards watching it
But now it's open for that person to see
They see you for who you really are
And you're riding high
You're telling them everything that you've been holding onto
You're letting go
Now you feel weightless
You can see yourself tell them all these things and you want yourself to stop talking however you don't
You tell them how great they are and what they mean to you
You tell them that there a treasure you're riding so high
You're flying in the sky
Now stop
Because if they don't feel the same about you, you're going to hit the ground hard

Fixed

Your beauty makes me shiver
I look at you in fascination
With the biggest line of inspiration, your beauty inspires me to
climb the highest mountain
with no equipment, no way down
Your beauty is a myth, but I believe in it
I believe in the shape of your face, the curve of the peak of your
nose,
the never-ending bright color of your eyes
The flaws on your face become an endless supply of perfection
If only you knew when you look in the mirror what I knew
when I gaze upon you my eyes fixed,
stuck in time,
in a delightful rhyme
Your beauty is a perfect song that I see inside my mind

If

The holocaust never happened,
No Indian, excuse me, Native American lost their land
World war one, two period never existed
No black person ever got pulled over by a police officer
Black people were never slaves
Everyone is equal
Everyone is equal
Hitler was never pissed off
What are you talking about?
The towers never fell
9/11 is just a date
There is no debate about gender
No talk of abortion
Women being raped never even crossed a newsfeed
Pedophiles isn't even a word in the dictionary
Everyone is equal
Everyone is equal
These are all things that I want to say to my four-year-old child,
so I struggle with those lies
Man, I wish we had the imagination he has because sometimes
it's fun to play if

Discover You

I want to wait for you
And make every second turn into a minute
Make every minute become one hour and every hour turn our
love into ecstasy
I want to hold your hand and get stuck in time to wear the rest
of the world goes by slow and the only reality is looking into
your eyes and getting lost for a lifetime
I want to hold your hand as though you were about to slip off
the edge
I want to kiss you like every kiss is a breath that I need to take as
though I was underwater and your kisses were oxygen
I want to know what makes you tick
I want to bend you, to thrill you, to enjoy you
I want to hold you and never let go of you
I want to say that I love you and make that word become
an entity so that when I'm a way from you, you always have
something to hold on to
Quite frankly, the gist of it all is that all I want to do is discover
you

Crying to the Deaf

Do you sense me when I'm in the room, lingering like a ghost? Maybe a smell of someone's great perfume, maybe the stench of a dead person that was stuffed into a mattress in a hotel room, unnoticeable.

Do you hear my voice booming through a speaker, bouncing off the sound waves, created by another scream of someone in shackles beaten and bruised by society?

Can you feel me like a child passing through its mother's womb, slowly creeping into the world, unknowing what's to come, still unnoticeable?

Do you see me? Do you see me?

No, you don't.

Standing in front of you, screaming out, yelling louder than any sound, but yet you don't hear me, you don't see me punching the walls, crawling up like I'm Spider-Man, yet I'm not able to hold on to myself.

I don't recognize me, so how can you recognize me?

Do you really see me pulling my skin off, scratching for a better person, to be noticed for who I am on the inside?

That person, dammit! Dammit all!

And what you assume, you see, because I'm not strong enough to hold on, and you're not strong enough to see me.

I picture that's the last thing my hero said before he took his own life.

Tough Cookie

(The Song of Angelina)

Do you want to get those hands?
Do you want to get these hands?
The first phrase I ever heard her say
When I was talking to her former friend on the line
And by line I mean assembly line.
I exchange words with her friend, I believe her name was Bree.
I gave her words, she gave me words, and we went our separate
ways.
Do you want to get these hands?
Words that she uses like throwing daggers always seem to hit
her target even without aim.
Do you want to get these hands?
Words that she uses as a shield against man
Who look her up and down lick their lips
Like she is a tall glass of water.
Do you want to get these hands?
She says to man
Because when they look at her, she knows that they only want
one thing.
Do you want to get these hands,
More than a question mark, more of an exclamation mark.

Do you want to get these hands?
She has her own engaging style.
Do you want to get these hands?
She won't fade.
Do you want to get these hands?
She has everything she needs.
So you want to get these hands?
She won't fold.
Do you want to get these hands?
She's invincible.
Do you want to understand these words that I gave to you?
I want her not to fight
She is just a delight
But it's not right for this to be the everyday fight
For a woman

Mystery I Assume

You are a supernatural night-light lighting the way on top of
the dark sea
The outline of your face was sketched by God's right hand
perfectly.
Your beauty is so flawless it's causing waves
And breaking thunder.
You are an illuminating anchor
That is keeping me fixated and safe so I don't float off into the
nothingness of space.

My Secret

(Part One)

I have found comfort in despair…
I made it my home, then out of nowhere, you appear.
You are a supernova of wonderful delight, a force of nature that is so out of sight…
So much power that you have one wave, or even with just a glance, I'm stuck in a trance if you only knew…
I hope for you, I pray for you
I wish for you to find all the happiness in the world…
When I talk to you, I get lost in your eyes
It always catches me by surprise…
The words I want to say to you I can't deny are the greatest words that I will ever speak…
I want you to pour out all your anger on me, everything that upsets you…
I want to kiss your forehead and wake up next to you…
If you asked me for light, I would set myself on fire
If I wasn't the one you wanted, I would wear a mask for you…
There's so much that I want for you…
Now, Nicole, if you excuse me, I need to go blend back in with despair.

Over You

Raindrops keep falling on my head
And I pretend like it's not supposed to hurt me but instead I'm happy
I'm happy with everything that I am
I'm happy accepting the pain
The pain of trying to breathe in a room that you sucked all the air out of
I'm happy embracing the negativity that you hurled at me as though I was a target because your bow is always aim toward me
I found happiness, and you can't take this, you can't walk on this
This is my cloud nine, and you had every chance to shape this, and by this, I mean my heart
But now it's too big to fit in the palm of your hand
You let your guard down, and that's how I was able to slip out of the crack to find my own happiness and this is a fact that I existed before you and I will exist after you.

Broken

We collide like two ships in the night with no lighthouse,
picking our brains every day so we don't go insane, thinking and hoping
that we know what the others think, but really, it's our own insecurities that reassure us
that we are not secure with ourselves, so we use our alibis
like a rockaby to paralyze
just to get by
off our own brokenness inside
how did two broken people meet in the night?
catch one another's eyes and get caught by surprise, but the truth is,
wow,
we are fighting ourselves
and not letting go of what's within
you know the truth
that I'm the missing piece to your heart, and you're the last piece to fix my spirit

Sidenote 6

When you allow someone else's actions to dictate your future and control your present, then you have given that person more power than you will ever know

Sidenote 10

I'm between hope and reality, dancing on that thin line of sanity
You have become my goal, and I drive toward you
Even though I know it will never be and it will crush me, I'm
still pushing forward, waiting to accept my failure

Sidenote 8

She makes comments like
"No one loves me that much"
If only she knew that my love for her is greater than the weight
of the earth

Sidenote 9

She is my universe, the start,
the end, my forever

My Inner Me Is My Enemy

My insides are hollow,
just a dusty reminiscence of what once was, which is fine because
I draw the line in the sand, and this is where I stand
that my inner me is my enemy.
Complexion, the outside is what we always see.
That's what we stand on and hold on to to set us free
Free from our own pain,
our own hatred,
so we judge one another without knowing one another, without
knowing what one man
and one woman is going through.
My inner me is my enemy,
my inner me is telling me that I'm fat,
I'm worthless,
so the next person I see
judge them for what I don't see.
Tell that man that he's not strong enough to stand,
tell that woman that her only worth is between her legs,
tell the child that his father left because of him.
My inner me is my enemy
My inner me is my enemy
I am not afraid of another man because he can't break me,
I'm not afraid of the words from a woman because she can't
shake me,
I'm more afraid of what I would do if I'm alone
because that would shape me.

My inner me is my enemy
My enemy is my inner me
That thing that's stopping me from loving my fellow man,
that thing that's causing me not to understand,
that thing that's causing me to rupture
and bleed out where I stand
My enemy may be my inner,
it's devastating that I hate you because I'm afraid of me

Verse Your Beauty

You got my mind racing
You got my heart pacing back and forth
But yet and still,
I can't even say shit, shush my mouth, hush up now
If I tell you the truth, I leave myself open
Like I'm lost out at sea, and I can't even swim
Can't you see that this is devastating for me?
You're the beauty from afar
Seems like I'm stocking you from my car, but I need to keep
my distance
If you ask me the truth, I shell, put up resistance
I shall commence to condense my feelings
Into nothing more than a smile
So hello from afar,
My angel of mine,
The messenger to the guiding light of the truth
That is useless to find in a vacuum of hope
You are so dope, but nope,
With no legs,
I'll pull myself up this rope to stand
And hold myself steady to try to be ready
To simply tell you no words
I know from my point of view it seems so absurd
But you are my beauty from afar

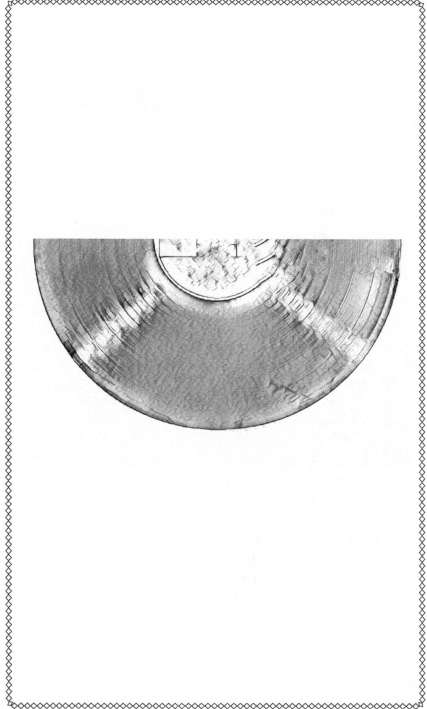

Broken Record

I, I, I
Crave you
Like you are the perfect drug at a rave
You are, are, are
The forbidden fruit that's hidden among thousands, thousands
of bad apples
We, we, we are both lonely
If only my inner thoughts weren't exposed,
I would love to pose a question that my naked, sinful, shameless
mind is dwelling on
Would you, would you, would you whip me?
No, skip that, forget that
X that out of your mind, if you don't mind
I'm in my thirties, and everything I say seems dirty
Wait a second, I meant to say, nerdy,
Shortly, I can talk to you without sweating, without repeating,
repeating, repeating,
Stop, listen,
You are the unlockable character in the video game of life

The Little Things

Every little thing is a big thing
Like your first step that you take as a child and your parents looked at you
There's so much rushing through their minds that if they didn't remember to breathe, they would forget…
Like the first time you rode a bike or flew a kite,
Noticing a spider crawling up your arm, so tiny,
So small,
But it makes your whole entire body jump…
Or that boy that you liked when you were in middle school when you saw him
Your hands would become all sweaty, and you felt something
In the pit of your stomach
That they later told you were butterflies…
What about the lies that were told to you that Santa Claus is real
And that the tooth fairy would collect your teeth under your pillow?
Oh, all those little things that we take for granted…
We forget about the beauty
And sitting on the beach, watching the sunset, being in nature, and been amazed by it.
Sitting alone in your car
And laughing because you remember a memory between you and a dear friend
You remember your first kiss
How it felt like you couldn't stand…
Or when your doctor told you that your mom beat cancer

You forgot about that memory
And how powerful it was
But what of the little thing that happened when your mom held
your hand
And she caught the tear that ran down your cheek…
That tear that left was a memory of pain leaving your body…
Like I said, every little thing is a big thing

Highly Evolved

If you're not living on the edge, you're taking up space
I see people beside me every day on the edge
Fearless,
Excited,
Not knowing what tomorrow will bring,
If they will be a hero or a villain in the story of life,
Not knowing that we are absentminded of our own spirits.
We don't know that the space we're standing in is vacant,
So we revolve around one another, holding fast not to fall.
No one knows how to live in the now,
Fearful that they may become the villain of the story,
So some of us amazingly grow a backbone and let go because
the hero will jump off to make room others.
What about those who evolved to revolve around them?
Now they must devolve back away from the edge.
Now they can't cheer for the breathtaking bravery of humanity.
What of the mind-blowing magic of hope?
The happy, fearless, delightful, spectacular triumph of victory
over hate.
We have to live on the edge, uplifting the wonderful struggles
that make us feel alive.
We have to dance with the beautiful demons from inside so that
the light on the outside shines bright.
We have to understand that we have to devolve into ourselves so
we can revolve around everyone else just to evolve to be greater
then what we are.
We all clash with something on the battlefield of life.
I put on my armor to battle the things we can't see.

You're In My Head

You're in my head, tormenting me
like a schoolyard bully
you know all the negative of me
counting all my flaws that are easy to see
You're in my head,
shaping me, molding me
into what you want me to be your puppet
without the string but everyone can see
there's no transparency
it's right in front of me
You're in my head, chained and shackled
I can't be mad I supplied them
I'm torturing myself with the memories of you, locked, playing
behind my eyes like moving pictures
Now how can I be mad when you are exactly where I want you
to be?
You're in my head, building me
Don't ever leave

Sidenote 5

Forgive me for I never knew that you existed
I've never had the opportunity to meet you
I missed it

About the Author

Karsten Colbert was born in Detroit, Michigan. He first discovered the art of poetry while reading Edgar Allan Poe's *The Tell-Tale Heart*. After that, he fell in love with spoken word poetry. Karsten was attending open mics and someone asked if he had any of his work published. The thought had never crossed his mind before attending open mics. Karsten had a fear of sharing his art with the world because he struggled with dyslexia. After that conversation opens up, a new level of fear to overcome—sharing his art with the world.

CPSIA information can be obtained
at www.ICGtesting.com
Printed in the USA
LVHW091925291020
669933LV00009B/468